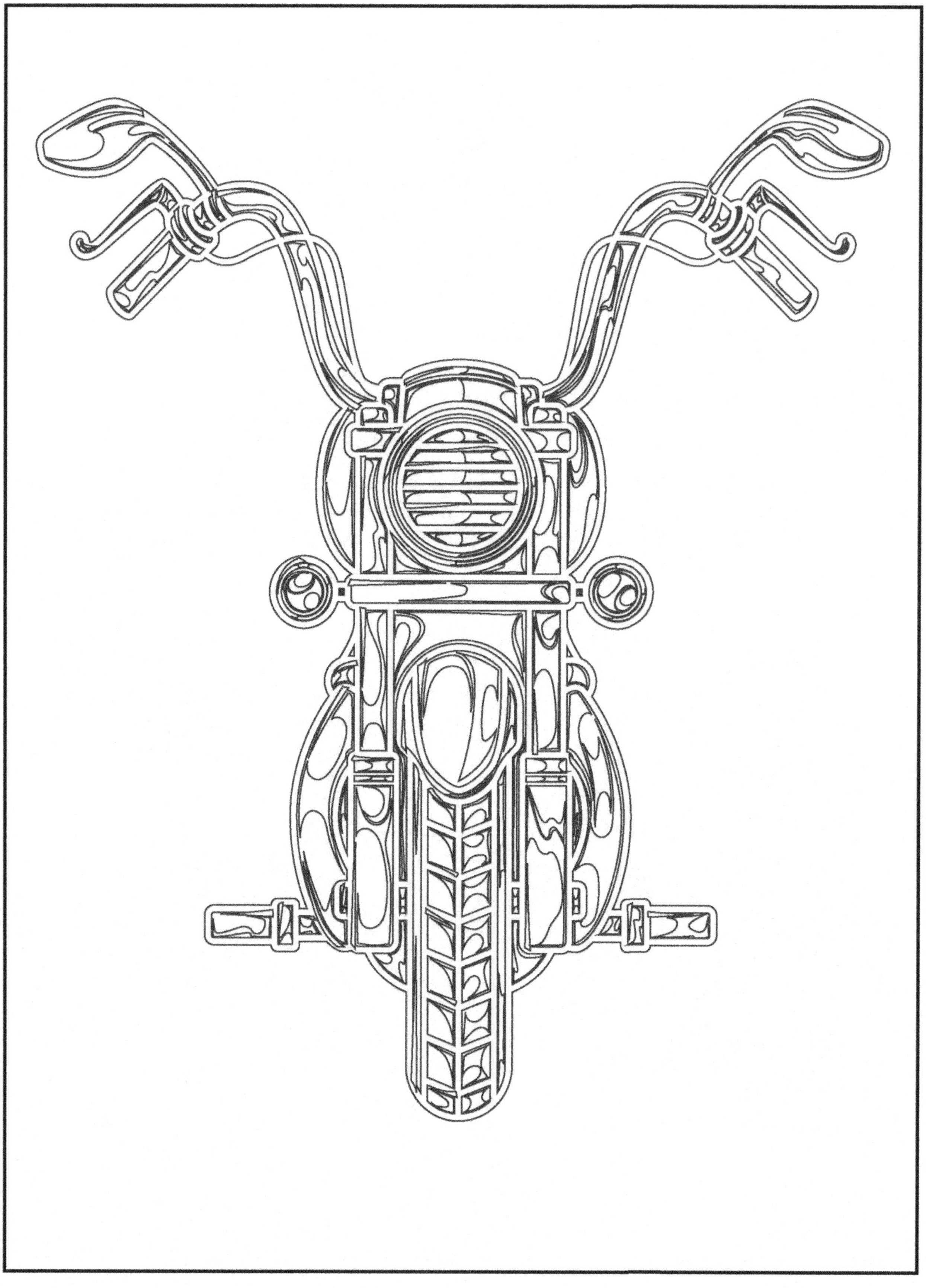

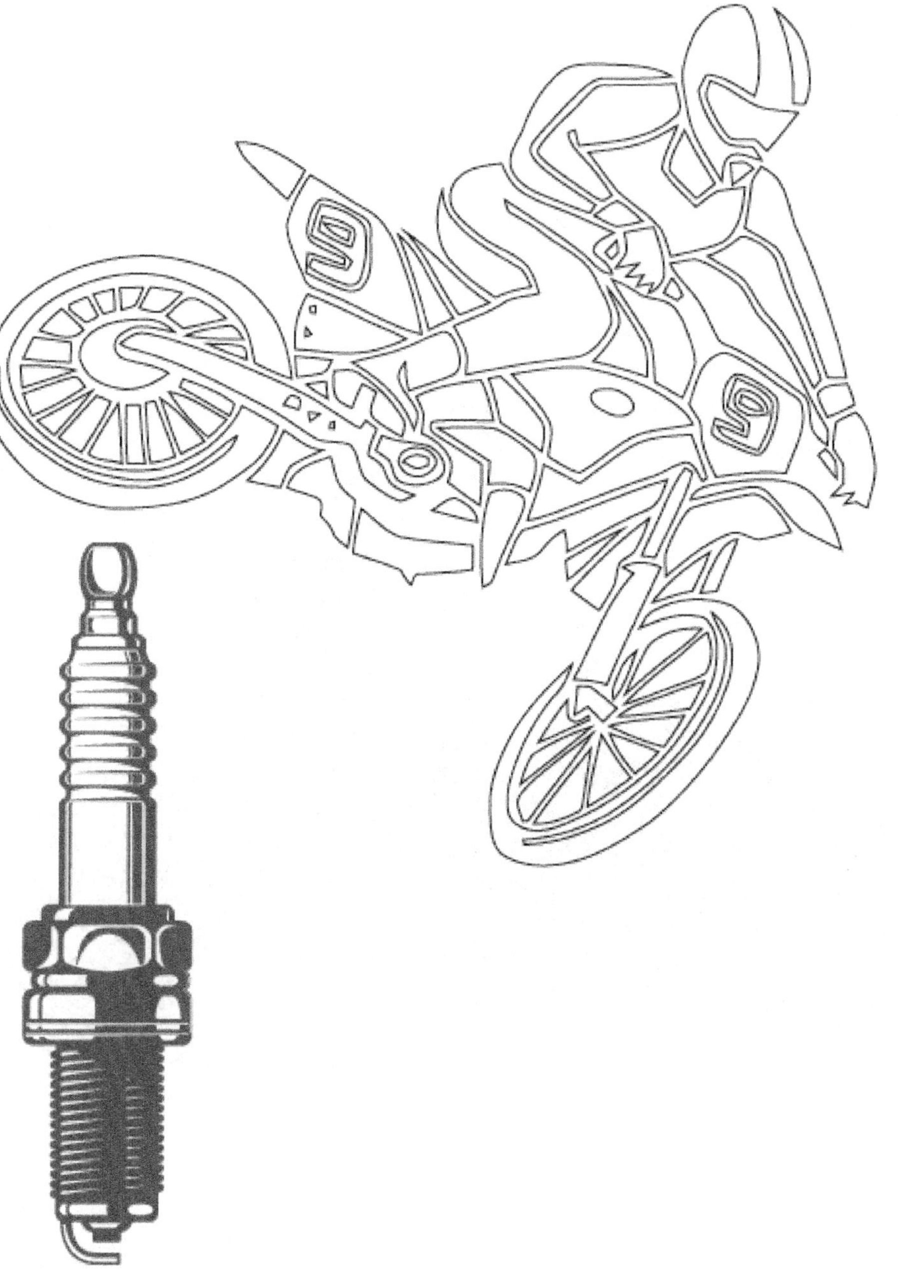
9
9

15

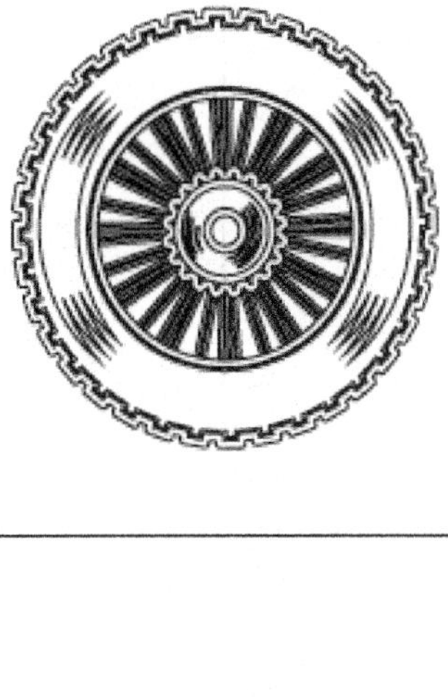

69

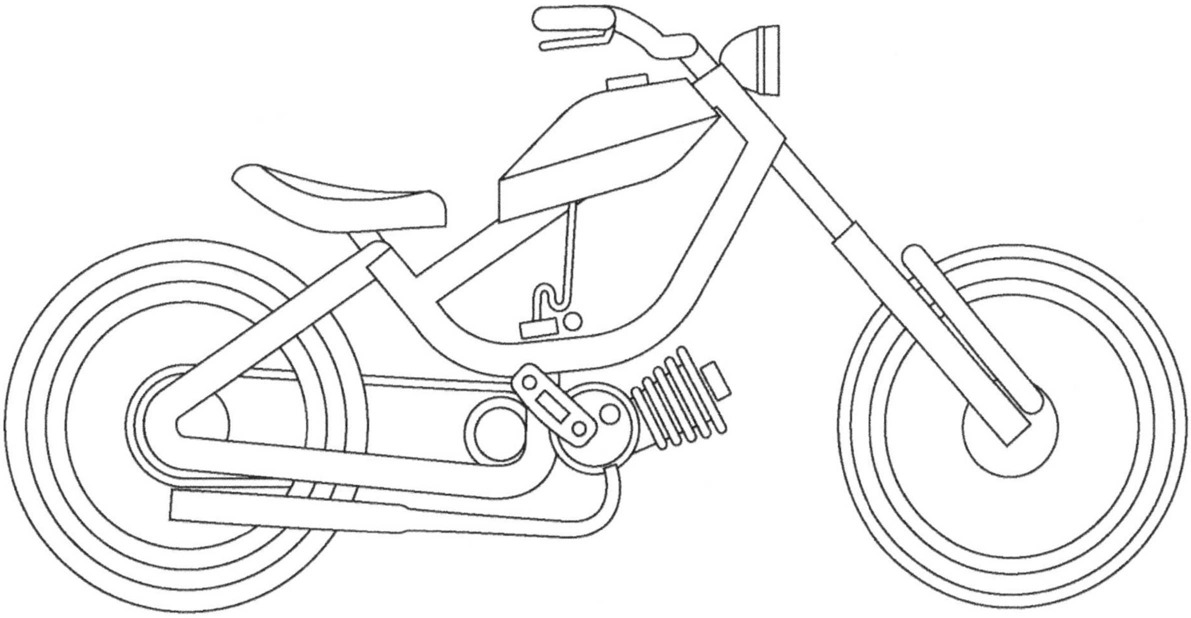

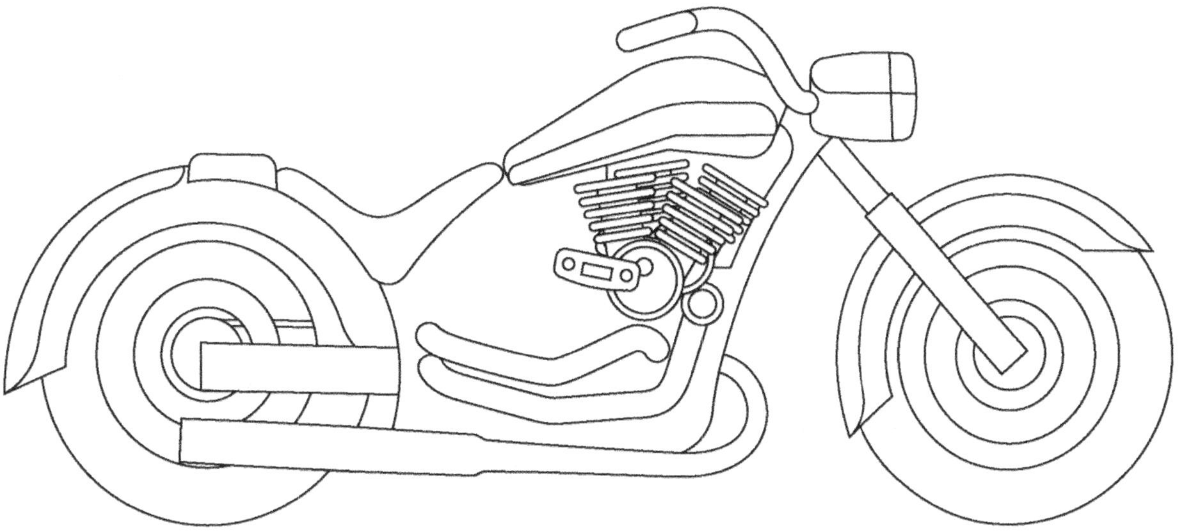

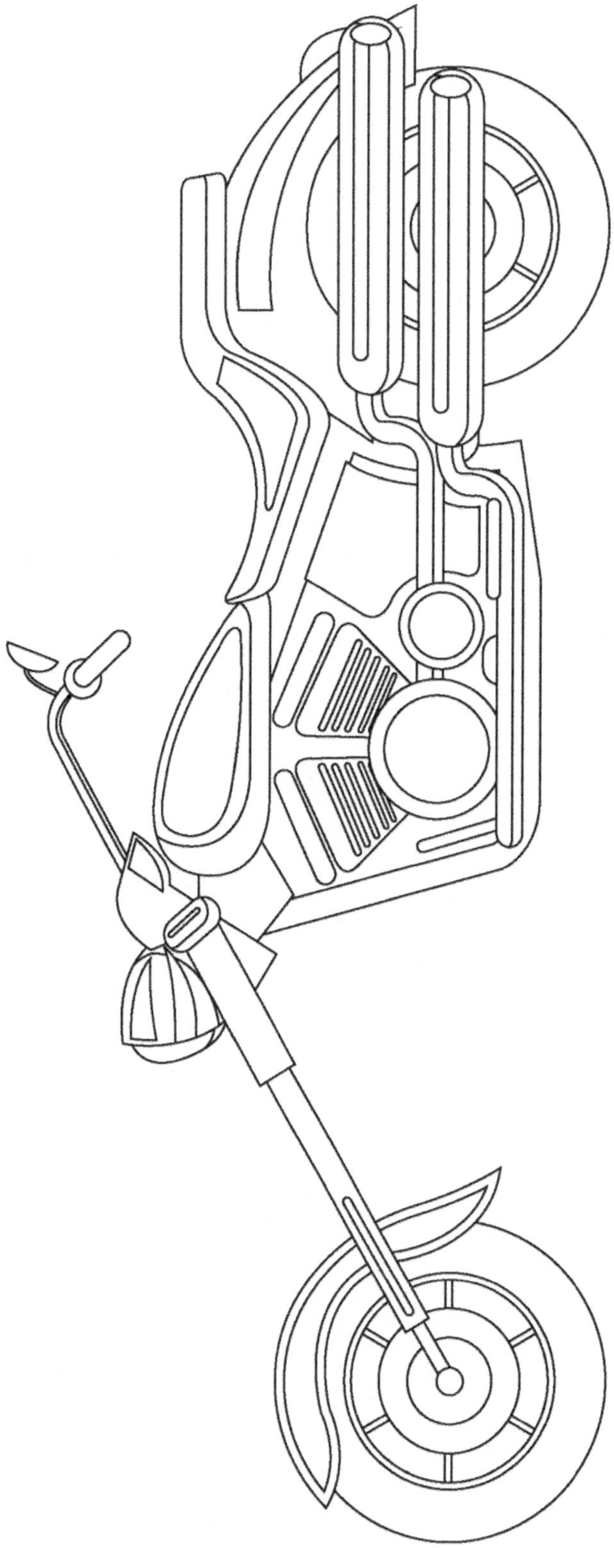

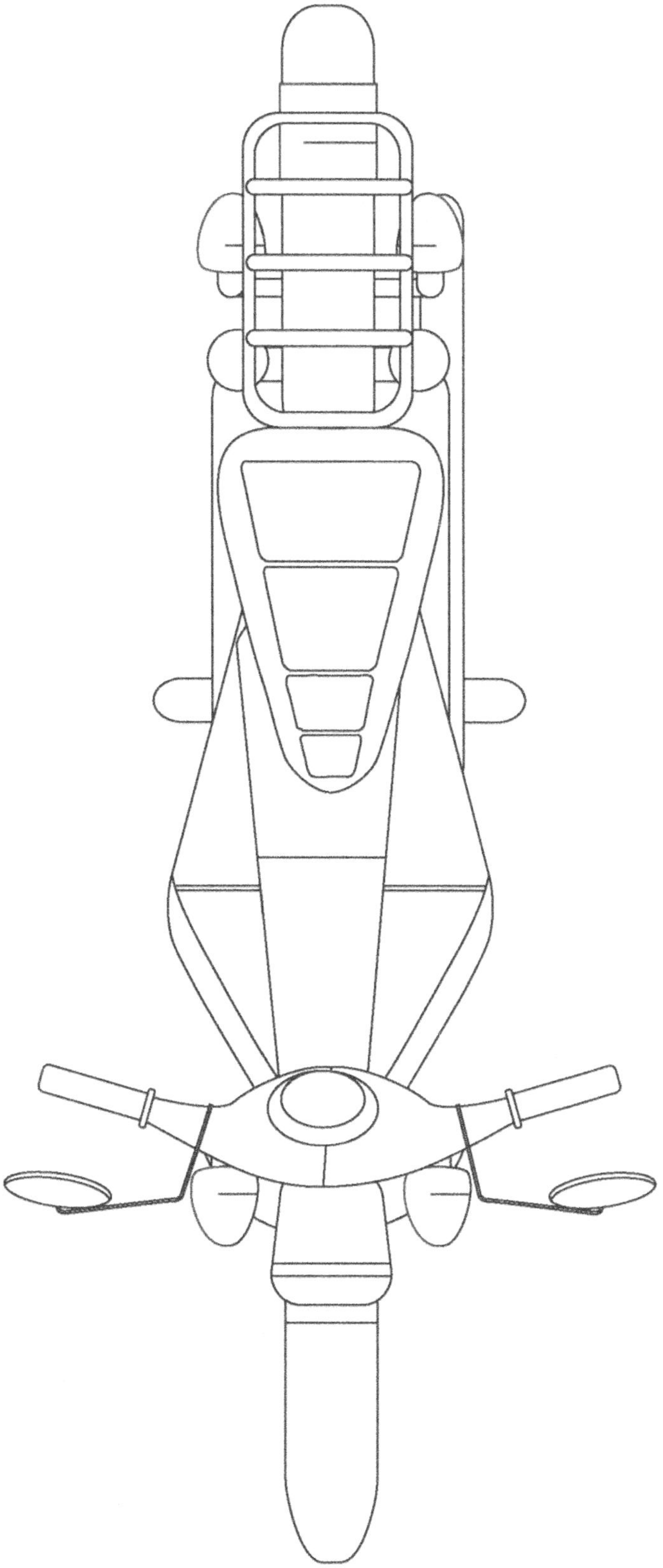

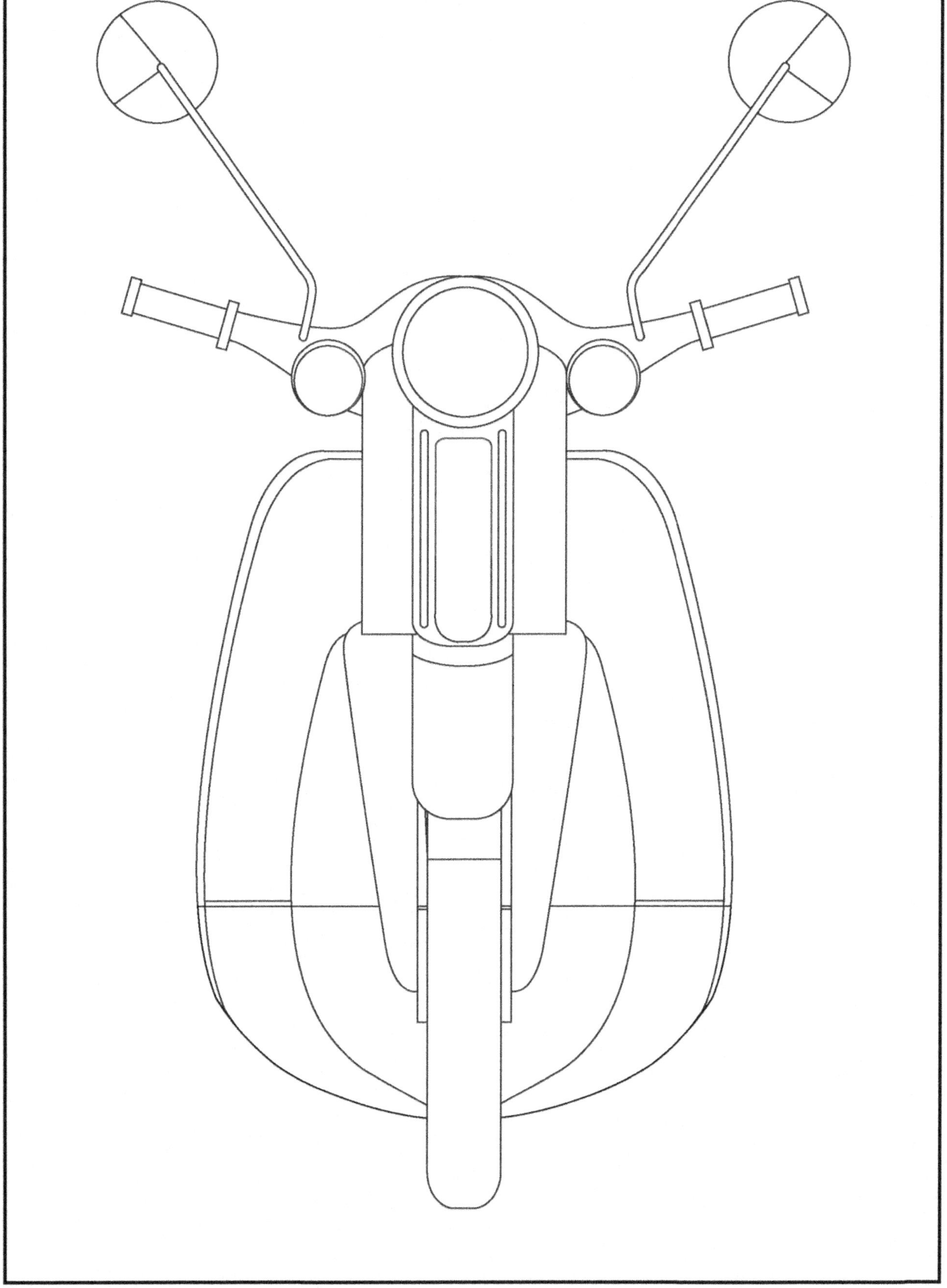

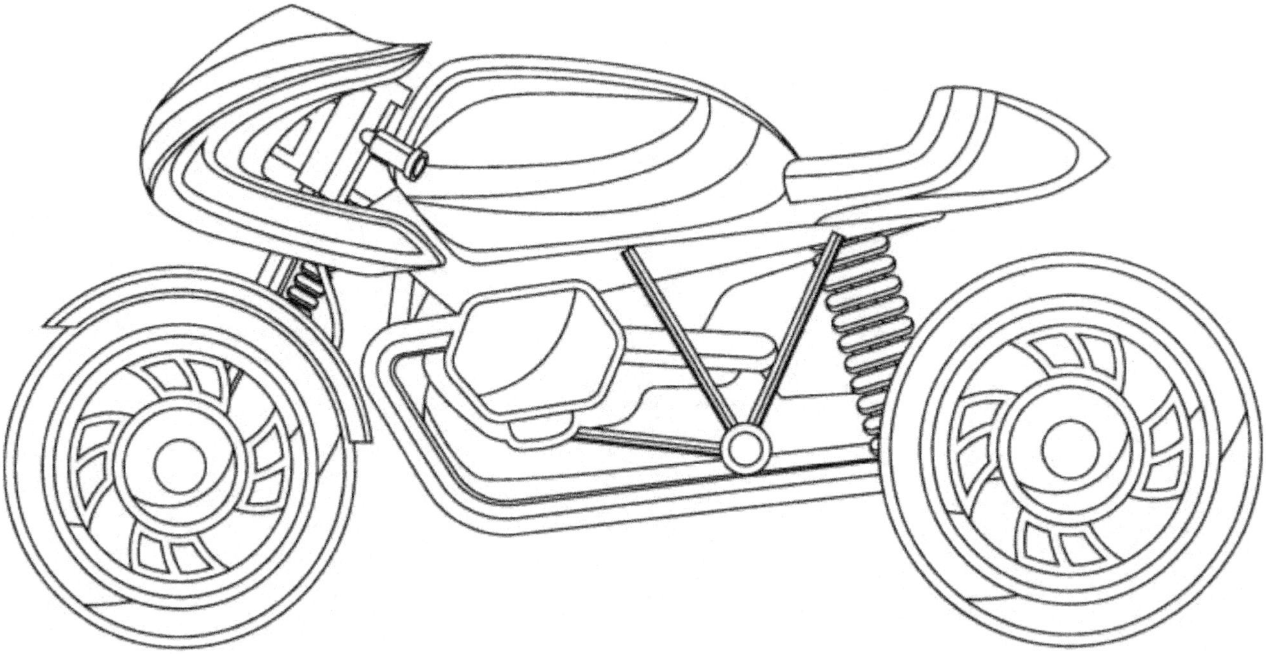

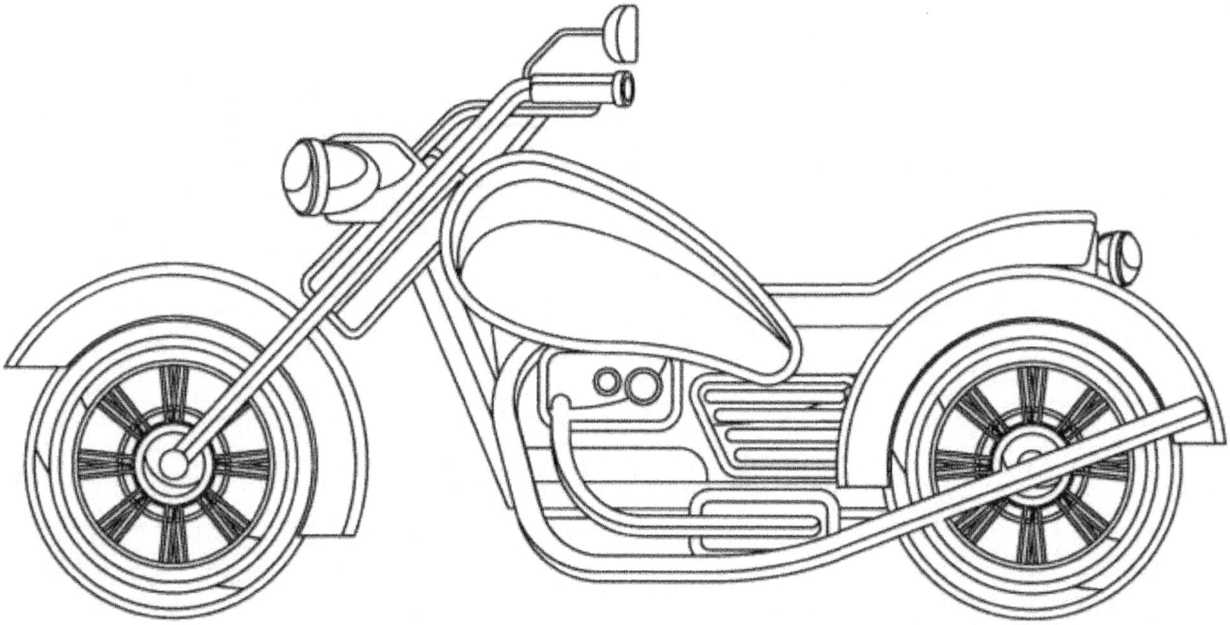

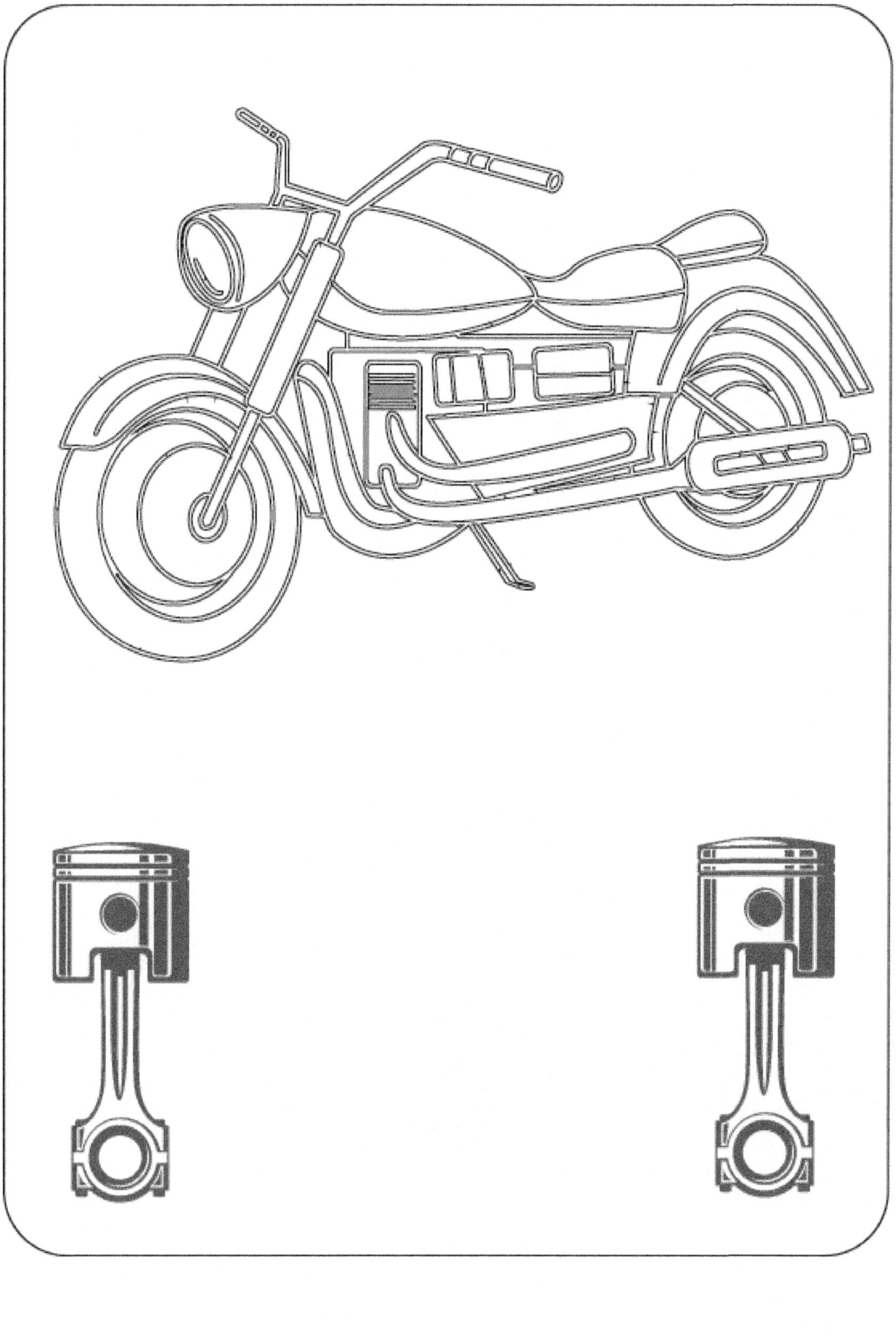

Made in the USA
Monee, IL
31 August 2021

76932117R00057